For Nick and our cubs, Harry, Joey, and Oscar
—*I. M. T.*

For my dear friend Amalia, a sunny, joyful companion
—*D. E.*

BLOOMSBURY CHILDREN'S BOOKS
Bloomsbury Publishing Inc., part of Bloomsbury Publishing Plc
1385 Broadway, New York, NY 10018

BLOOMSBURY, BLOOMSBURY CHILDREN'S BOOKS, and the Diana logo are trademarks of Bloomsbury Publishing Plc

First published in Great Britain in October 2020 by Bloomsbury Publishing Plc
Published in the United States of America in November 2021 by Bloomsbury Children's Books

Text copyright © 2020 by Isabel Thomas
Illustrations copyright © 2020 by Daniel Egnéus

Bloomsbury books may be purchased for business or promotional use. For information on bulk purchases please contact Macmillan Corporate and Premium Sales Department at
specialmarkets@macmillan.com

Library of Congress Cataloging-in-Publication Data
available upon request
ISBN: 978-1-5476-0692-4 (hardcover) • ISBN: 978-1-5476-0693-1 (e-book)

Printed and bound in China by Leo Paper Products Ltd
2 4 6 8 10 9 7 5 3 1 (hardcover)

To find out more about our authors and books visit www.bloomsbury.com and sign up for our newsletters.

Fox

A Circle of Life Story

Isabel Thomas   Daniel Egnéus

BLOOMSBURY
CHILDREN'S BOOKS
NEW YORK LONDON OXFORD NEW DELHI SYDNEY

The ground is frozen.
The branches are bare.
Dead leaves crunch underfoot.

But look closely. Listen carefully.
Life is stirring in the shadows.

A bushy tail.
A flash of fire.
The soft pad of sooty paws.

Follow fox.
Ears pricked, nose to ground,
she's caught a scent.
Don't make a sound.

Rabbits nibble fresh
green shoots.
Then freeze.

Ears stiffen.
Noses twitch.

Fox creeps,
then leaps!

An arc of rust-red fur.

But her prey has gone.
Fox pads on.

Follow fox through the trees,
between the railings, along the road.
While the city rests,
fox finds food that doesn't move.

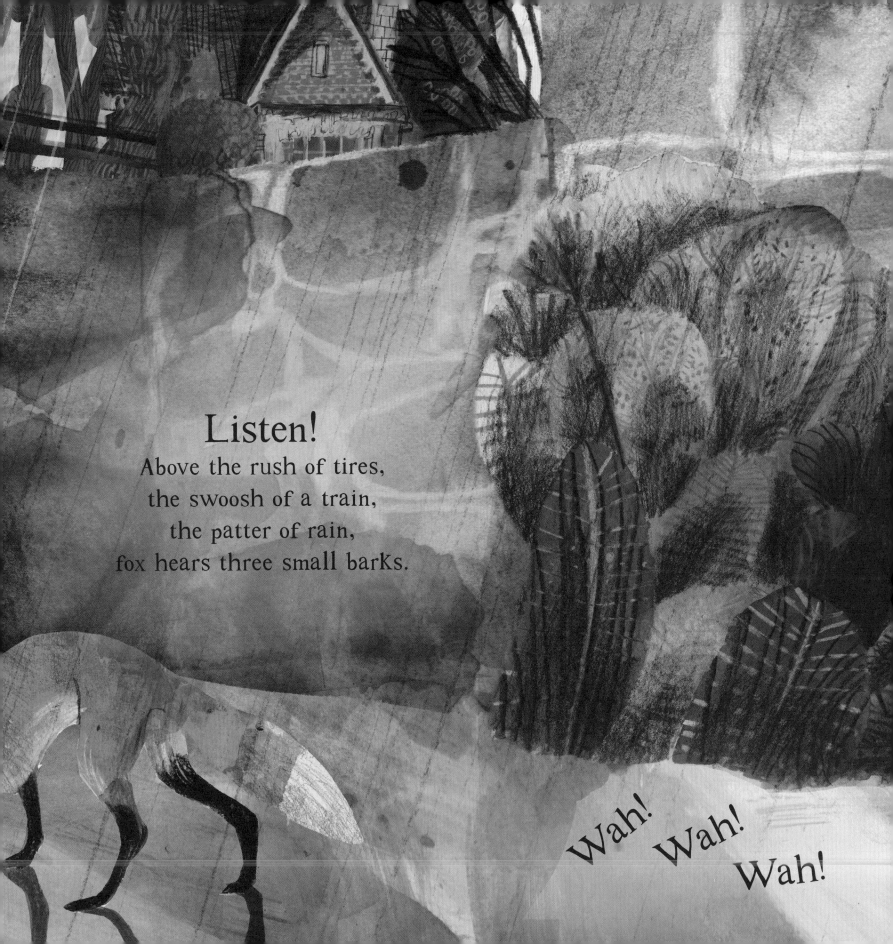

Listen!
Above the rush of tires,
the swoosh of a train,
the patter of rain,
fox hears three small barks.

Wah! Wah! Wah!

Follow fox
under the fence,
across the garden,
and into her dark den—

where fuzzy gray cubs
wait for their feast.
From bird, from plants,
from water, from air
flow the things foxes need
to live and grow.

In a few weeks,
the cubs are bigger, bolder.
They are ready to play.
Near their den,
where it's safe,

they somersault,
chase, and stumble,

tug of war,
rough and tumble.

Head over tail,
geKKering as they go.

While the cubs wait for fox
to bring back food,
they play at being hunters.

Devouring earthworms,

bulldozing beetles,

and snapping at insects.

Soon it's time to test their skills.

Follow fox

under the fence,

along the road,

between the railings,

and through the trees.

Watch fox.
Ears pricked, nose to ground,
she's caught a scent.
Don't make a sound.

Success!
After playing tug of war,
hungry fox cubs hunt for more.
Until . . .

. . . fox hears a strange new sound.

Waaaohhh!

Follow fox.
Run back home.

Three cubs dash across the road
to safety on the other side.

But fox gets caught in dazzling lights.

The car brakes.
Too late.

And fox is thrown . . .

. . . into tangled grass.

Fox curls up,
her heartbeat slows,
her last breath hangs in the air.

Three cubs look around,
sniff the ground,
hesitate . . .

then pad back home.

As summer turns to autumn
and fallen leaves decay . . .

. . . tiny creatures get to work
and fox begins to fade away.

Back to earth, to plants, to air
flow the tiny particles
that were once a fox.

Mites and magpies
take their share.

Flies and beetles visit too,
laying their eggs
where they know

brand-new life can
feed and grow.

Just as winter turns to spring,
new life flows from old.
As every particle that once was fox
finds a new place in the world . . .

. . . in grass, in trees, in rabbits, in bees,
in daffodils dancing in the breeze.

When the world seems still
and the branches are bare
and dead leaves lie all around—

look closely. Listen carefully.

Life is everywhere.

Death is not just an end,
but a beginning.

What happens when something dies?

Life on Earth is remarkable. Almost nine million different species of animals, plants, and other living things share our planet. A fox, a fir tree, and a fungus may seem very different from one another, but they are made of the same ingredients—the building blocks of life.

The building blocks of life

Just as hundreds of thousands of words can be spelled with the same 26 letters, all living things are made up of about thirty fundamental particles, combined in different ways. Living things need a supply of these particles to survive, to grow bigger, and to repair injuries. Plants get them from air, water, and soil. They use the energy from sunlight to turn particles into food. Animals get them from air, water, and the food they eat. When animals eat other animals, these fundamental particles are passed along, too. They are the building blocks of life.

What is death?

It seems strange, but death is a part of the cycle of life on Earth. Living plants and animals breathe, move, grow, feed, get rid of waste, reproduce, sense, and respond to the world around them. When a living thing dies, these processes stop. The plant or animal no longer breathes, moves, grows, or feels what is happening around them. Only the building blocks of life are left behind. After a life ends, a process called decomposition begins. This recycles the particles so they can be used by other living things.

What is decomposition?

Decomposition is a natural process that begins inside the cells of a plant or animal that was once alive. Millions of tiny creatures, called microbes, live on and inside plants and animals. These microbes do all sorts of useful jobs while a plant or animal is alive. When it dies, the microbes begin breaking it down and releasing the building blocks of life back into the environment. This doesn't hurt the plant or animal because it is not alive anymore.

Lots of different creatures help with decomposition, too. Invertebrates such as mites and earthworms, and larger creatures such as scavenging birds, use the dead plant or animal for food.

Insects visit to lay eggs. When the eggs hatch, their larvae will have the energy and nutrients they need to live and grow. The dead plant or animal becomes a mini ecosystem buzzing with new life that is nourished by the old life.

The work done by each decomposer is tiny, but together they play a very important role in the cycle of life. As they feed and grow, decomposers also respire (breathe) and produce waste of their own. This returns nutrients to the air and soil, where they can be used by other plants and animals.

The cycle of life

Like dead leaves that have fallen from a tree in autumn, a dead plant or animal will gradually disappear, but its particles do not vanish. They are returned to the soil and the air. They are soaked up by roots and taken in by leaves, becoming a part of new leaves, flowers, branches, and seeds. They are passed up the food chain, where they may become a part of bees buzzing in a garden or birds soaring in the sky. In nature, nothing goes to waste.

Death is not just an end

No single plant or animal lives forever, but decomposition means that their particles will go on to be a part of new life. Just as water cycles from clouds to the sea and back to the sky, the building blocks of life are constantly on the move, from the environment to living, moving, breathing creatures, and back again.

A death is the end of one life, but it is also the beginning of many more.